YOUTHREPRENEURS 4 LIFE

I0482014

About the Author

Miss Lei'Lani White is the founder of Youthreprenerurs 4 Life as well as a motivational speaker and an author. In April '2016, she was named as the chairperson for her middle school's chapter of the National Junior Honor Society for outstanding academic achievement. She was also one of ten Girl of Merit Award recipients in the state of North Carolina for academic performances, her commitment to community service and other causes and activities that she has been involved in and outside of Wake Young Women's Leadership Academy, where she is currently enrolled. She has tutored children at several after school programs.

She is also the co-founder of the Warriors 4 Epilepsy where she advocates for the Epilepsy cause by spreading awareness and by also performing in numerous events. She has also partnered with the Durham Epilepsy Support Team as a volunteer for many of their events and walks. Her mission is to make an impact in the lives of other youth.

Contents

ASPIRE 2 ACQUIRE

Strive, Soar & Succeed

05 The Importance of Financial Planning

08 Making Wise Financial Decisions

09 The Economy & How it Affects You

11 Preparing a Personal Budget

13 Savings and Investments

15 Banking Accounts and Services

16 Spending: Being a Responsible Consumer

17 Identity Theft

20 Community Service and Giving

22 Youthrepreneurship and Business Planning

Message from the Author

This guide presents the necessary tools needed to prepare, deliver, and engage youth who are being exposed to the world of financial literacy and entrepreneurship. By supporting youth throughout this learning process, this guide will give them an invaluable opportunity to understand how their choices about education, career, and managing money, and small business planning affects their overall well being and their family throughout their lives.

This guide will also give young people a sense of direction as they take several paths into their business journey. We hope that the outcome leaves them with a renewed sense of vision and purpose for their life!

I am 14 and I look forward to more endless possibilities, and leaving more footprints in the sand so that others can follow.

Lei'Lani S. White

CEO, Youthrepreneurs 4 Life

The Importance of Financial Planning

What exactly is financial planning?

Key Words

Financial Security

Goals
short-term goal
mid-range goal
long-term goal

Financial Plan

SHORT-TERM GOALS
1 YEAR

MID-TERM GOALS
1 - 5 YEARS

LONG-TERM GOALS
5+ YEARS

Good financial planning is the key to achieving **financial security**. In this unit, you will learn about financial goals and how to set them. You will also discover how the global economy affects you individually.

Financial security is what someone has achieved when they know that they can make, save, and invest enough money to achieve their goals.

Goals are some things that you really want to achieve

Financial Plan shows a person where they currently are in their finances and where they would like to go.

Strategies for Life

Taking a realistic view of your financial situation will help you now and in the future. There are many roads to achieving your goals. Find the right path for you.

A **forecast** is a prediction of what might happen in the future.

A **budget** is a plan for how to spend, save, and invest the money you make

Unemployment occurs when there are a number of people who are out of work and looking for a job.

An **economic indicator** is a number that tells you something about how the economy is performing..

GOAL SETTING ACTIVITIES

1. What are some of your short-term goals?

----

2. What goals you would like to achieve by the time you are 18 years old?

----

3. What goals would you like to achieve by the time you are 21? By the time you are 25? By the time you are 30?

----

4. What are some other goals you'd like to accomplish throughout your life? How do you plan to achieve them?

----

5. Make a wish list for what you would like to buy at different ages. At each age, tell how you will earn the money to save for the item on your wish list.

Making Wise Financial Decisions

A **financial plan** identifies a person's financial goals, and suggests ways of achieving those goals. It is also a roadmap for sound financial decision-making throughout his or her life.

What are some of your short-, medium-, and long-term goals? Are they realistic and possible to achieve, or are they just "wishful thinking?" To be sure your goals are sound, here are some steps you can take to make smart financial decisions:

a. **Review your current financial situation.**
a. **What is your total income? (money you earn from your allowance, babysitting, mowing lawns, and so on)**
c. **What expenses repeat, or recur, every month? (club dues, for example)**

THE ECONOMY & HOW IT AFFECTS YOU

The **economy** is the financial structure, or make-up, of a country.

When an economy is strong and is growing fast, prices usually start going up. This is called **inflation**. When prices fall, it can cause a **recession,** or trimming down of the economy.

During a recession, there are not enough jobs for everyone who wants to work. The rate of inflation and the **unemployment rate** are two economic indicators that affect how the economy behaves. **Economic indicators** include such things as how businesses are doing, unemployment rates, home sales, price increases or decreases (inflation/deflation), industrial production, stock market prices, and much more.

Take a look at the most recent recession in the U.S. and how it has affected families personally.

1. Did this period of economic decline cause your family to cut back or delay purchases?

2. Did they save more for a "rainy day?"

3. How else did it affect you?

ECONOMY WORKSHEET

Circle the correct answer for each of the questions below.

An economy is:

a. The supply of money in a country
b. The financial structure of a country
c. A country's unemployment rate

2. If the rate of inflation is high...
a. Prices are going down
b. Prices are going up
c. It's a good time to buy bonds

3. What kind of economy does the U.S. have?
a. A free-market economy
b. A government-controlled economy
c. An industrial economy

Preparing a Personal Budget

In this section, youth will learn how to prepare a monthly budget, which will include comparing their actual expenses (money they spend) versus what they forecast, or predict for a month. They will also learn about the types of accounts and services offered by banks. Finally, they will learn about how interest makes their money grow over time.

As stated earlier, a budget helps you keep track of how much you earn and how much you spend. Basically, it's a plan for how to spend, save, and invest the money you make. Preparing a personal monthly budget helps you keep track of your income (earnings) and expenses so that you can manage your money.

One of the easiest and most convenient places to keep your money is in a **bank**. Not only do banks offer you a variety of services, they also provide safety and security for your hard-earned money.

Finally, you will learn about a very important concept in this section which is the **Time Value of Money**. A dollar you have today may be worth more or less in the future, depending on how you invest it. The relationship between time, money, and **return on investment**, or ROI (for example, the interest you earn on your savings account), is called the time value of money.

A **budget** is a plan for how to spend, save, and invest the money you make. It helps you keep track of how much you earn and how much you spend.

Money you receive, such as what you make from a job, an allowance, or even gifts, is called **income**. Money you spend on school supplies, clothes, food, birthday gifts, and entertainment is called **expenses**.

If you spend more than you earn, you will have a **budget deficit**, or loss. If you spend less than you earn, you will have a **budget surplus**, or gain.

BUDGET DEFICIT

MONTHLY INCOME	$45.00
MONTHLY EXPENSES	55.00
DIFFERENCE (INCOME - EXPENSES)	(-$10.00)

BUDGET SURPLUS

MONTHLY INCOME	$55.00
MONTHLY EXPENSES	45.00
DIFFERENCE (INCOME - EXPENSES)	$10.00

SAVINGS AND INVESTING

Saving money is one of the most important steps toward financial security. When a person saves, he or she puts money aside on a regular basis. They put the money someplace safe, such as a **bank** or a **credit union**, so that it is available when they need it for an unexpected expense (such as when a bike has a flat tire) or a planned expense (such buying supplies at the beginning of the school year). As a bonus, the bank pays people **interest** just for putting the money in their account. The longer it stays in their account, the more money they will have to spend later.

Individuals may also decide to invest some of their money. Perhaps you can work with a parent to buy the stock of a company whose products you like. **Investing**, however, is riskier than saving because the deposit is usually not insured, and the amount of money one can earn is not guaranteed. It is even possible that someone can lose all of the money they invest. Nonetheless, investing gives people the chance to earn more money or to increase their savings at a faster rate.

Both saving and investing gives people a chance to increase their wealth, which can result in greater financial security and independence.

Saving keeps their money safe and available, and **investing** gives people the chance to make their money grow faster.

The amount someone saves and the amount they invest depends on their financial goals and resources, how old they are, and how much risk they are willing to take.

BANKING ACCOUNTS AND SERVICES

Income is money that you earn from work or receive as a gift.

Savings is money you set aside to reach a goal.

· A **savings account** is money kept in a bank or other financial institution.

· A **checking account** is a bank account against which the depositor can draw checks.

· A **deposit** is money you put into your savings account.

· You also earn **interest** on your savings. Interest is the amount the bank pays you each month for the use of your money so that they can make loans.

To open or add to your savings account, you make a deposit. A savings account provides safety for your money. Money in a bank is safe—even if the bank goes out of business. This is so because the government guarantees your deposits. If you do not save or invest your money, there is no protection if it is lost or stolen.

Let the buyer beware means you should always "look before you buy." It is your responsibility, not the seller's, to be informed about what you are buying and whom you are buying it from. Most people search the Internet today before they make a major purchase; checking for product reviews, comparing prices, and learning which sellers can be trusted.

A **consumer** is anyone who buys something. Consumer protection laws seek to stop consumers from being taken advantage of by businesses. Every state has consumer protection laws and an agency to enforce them. **The Federal Trade Commission** (FTC) watches businesses to be sure they do not use "unfair or deceptive practices" or use misleading or false advertising.

Consumer protection laws forbid businesses from lying about prices and from using advertising to fool people. These laws allow consumers who have been cheated to sue the business they believe has wronged them.

IDENTITY THEFT

Identity theft is a serious crime. If you are an identity theft victim, your ability to get a loan or use a credit card could suffer. Identity theft involves someone pretending to be someone else in order to steal their money or to get other benefits. A **credit rating** indicates how likely you are to repay money that you've borrowed. A **credit report** is a record of your history of borrowing and repaying debt. To minimize your chances of becoming an identity theft victim, do the following:

· **DETER** identity thieves by keeping your information safe.
· **DETECT** suspicious activity by regularly checking your financial accounts and billing statements.
· **DEFEND** against ID theft as soon as you suspect there's a problem by notifying your bank and credit card companies.

TIME AND MONEY WORKSHEET

1. Your Financial Goals

List two of your financial goals.

a. Goal #1: _____

b. Goal #2: _____

2. Time

What is the amount of time you have to save money for each goal?

a. Goal #1: _____

b. Goal #2: _____

3. Money

How much money do you think you'll need for each goal?

a. Goal #1: _____

b. Goal #2: _____

4. Planning for the Future

What is your plan for reaching each goal?

a. Goal #1: _____

b. Goal #2: _____

COMMUNITY SERVICE AND GIVING

It is important for you as young people to understand the many benefits of giving their time, talent, and money to good causes. **Philanthropy** involves helping out other people, be it volunteering at a soup kitchen, library, or animal shelter. Philanthropy can also involve giving money or goods, such as donating cans of food to a homeless shelter. Even when someone doesn't have money to give, they almost always have time and skills that they can share.

Community service is concern for the welfare of others in your community. When someone volunteers, they work on behalf of others or for a particular cause without payment. **Volunteering** is intended to improve the quality of life for all concerned.

The moral of the story here is that everyone has something to give that could help make the world a better place.

Philanthropy is a big word about something very important. Philanthropy is giving your time, skills, or money to help other people. Philanthropy includes volunteering at a soup kitchen or an animal shelter or giving money or cans of food to a homeless shelter, just to name a few ways to give back to your community.

A **nonprofit** is an organization that tries to improve society. Unlike other businesses, its main goal is not making money. It is called a "nonprofit" because it is not trying to make a profit. Your local library, for example, is a nonprofit.

A **foundation** is an organization that collects money and resources from businesses and people and gives them to nonprofits. The nonprofits use the money and resources to help make the world a better place.

A **mission statement** is a sentence or two that explains what a foundation or nonprofit does.

Many of the things we take for granted such as libraries, museums, a sculpture on the street, hospitals, land, etc.,—are supported all or in part by gifts of money, time, and effort

Youthrepreneurship and Business Planning

Good financial planning and goal setting are the keys for achieving financial security. And, they are all necessary ingredients for **BUSINESS PLANNING.**

Whether you want to prepare a delicious meal or purchase something, it should require planning.

This is a great affirmation to apply to your goals:
Proper Planning Prevents Poor Performance.

Your goals should be used as a **roadmap** to counter-attack **roadblocks**. There are some things that hinder or prevent people from pushing forward or even completing the tasks that they had once made a commitment towards.

Determination will give you the resolve to keep going in spite of the roadblocks that lay before you.

What is a Youthrepreneur

According to Webster's Dictionary, an **entrepreneur** is one who organizes, manages, and assumes the risks of a business or enterprise.

So, a **YOUTHREPRENEUR** is the same as above, except they are young children like you and me!

Before you set out on your business journey, there are some steps that you have to take.

What are your personal strategies for improvement and how do you gain these characteristics of a successful entrepreneur?

The very first step is to find out what you are passionate about and what your niche is.

What is a niche?

According to Webster's Dictionary, a **niche** is: a place, job, or use for which a person or a thing is best fitted. In other words, it is something that you are very passionate about and something that you won't get bored doing. It is something that you are already knowledgable about and that you can call yourself an expert at doing. Your niche and your passions can be a combination of your interests, beliefs, ethos, values, talents and skills, among a number of other characteristics.

Having a niche can also help you to identify your brand. Once you discover and identify your personal brand, you'll be ready to learn how to brand yourself.

What problems do you want to solve?

Focus on a problem that you're good at solving. You don't have to be the best, but you just need to be better than others at what you're trying to solve. As long as you have a reasonable level of knowledge, expertise and skills, then you will be fine.

TYPES OF BUSINESS STRUCTURES

The most common forms of business structures are:

Sole Proprietorship
Sometimes a person gets tired of working for someone else and then they decide to be their own boss. This business structure is the easiest to start a business with a minimum of hassle and expense. Another advantage of a sole proprietorship is that all of the after-tax profits go to the single owner of the business.

Unlimited liability is one of the major disadvantages of having a sole proprietorship. Your small business, in the form of a sole proprietorship, is personally liable for all debts and actions of the company.

The owner of a sole proprietorship is solely liable for all debts and actions of the company. All personal wealth is linked to the business. Financial statements are not required in a sole proprietorship as are typically required of a corporation, meaning a lack of financial control is very probable.

It is difficult to find outside investors to fund sole proprietorships, meaning growth potential is very limited beyond a certain point.

Partnership

A **limited partnership** is a partnership with one or more general partners and one or more limited partners.

A limited partner in this type of business invests money in the partnership but does not have any management responsibilities or any liability for losses beyond the initial investment. A general partner takes an active role in managing the partnership and accepts unlimited liability for the firm's losses.

In a **general partnership** all partners have unlimited liability for the debts of the firm. If the firm goes bankrupt or loses a lawsuit, the partners can lose personal assets such as their homes or cars. To make matters worse, each partner is liable for these debts no matter who was responsible for incurring them.

Limited Liability Company (LLC)

The owners of a limited liability company have limited liability for the debts of their company meaning that the members of the company cannot be held personally liable for the company's debts or liabilities.

They may also choose to be taxed either as a partnership or as a corporation. And, unlike an S corporation, there is no limit on the number of investors or their citizenship and residence.

C Corporation

Ownership in a **C corporation** may be held by a large number of people who do not take an active role in managing the company. Ownership of a corporation is represented by shares of stock, and the people who own the stock are called **stockholders**. Though stockholders have the right to elect a board of directors, and thus exert some influence on how the firm is managed, many stockholders take no further role in working for or managing the company they own.

One of the main disadvantages of C corporations is **double taxation**. This means that the earnings of a C corporation are taxed first as corporate income. Then any profits paid as dividends to stockholders are taxed again as income of the stockholder.

S Corporation

One requirement of an S corporation is that all individual stockholders must be U.S. citizens or permanent residents of the United States. An s corp offers investment opportunities, perpetual existence, and that coveted protection of limited liability. But, unlike a c corp, s corps only have to file taxes yearly and they are not subject to double taxation.

Nonprofit Corporation

A **Nonprofit corporation** is a special type of corporation that has been organized to carry out a charitable, educational, religious, literary or scientific purpose. A nonprofit can raise funds by receiving public and private grant money and donations from individuals and companies. Not all nonprofits are **tax-exempt**, and not all tax-exempt organizations are charities.

To qualify for Nonprofit status, your corporation must be formed to benefit:
(1) the public,
(2) a specific group of individuals, or
(3) the membership of the Nonprofit.

Examples of Nonprofits include: religious organizations, charitable organizations, political organizations, credit unions and membership clubs such as the Elk's Club or a country club.

Reasons to Form a Nonprofit Corporation

As someone involved with a charitable cause, you might be weighing the benefits of formally organizing your nonprofit. Sure, it will take a little extra work, but only with a state-recognized nonprofit corporation can you obtain private and public grants, low-cost postage rates and be exempt from income, sales and property taxes. Most importantly, only a formal nonprofit corporation allows individuals to donate money tax-free, while shielding your personal assets from liability. If you decide to form a nonprofit corporation, there are a few documents that you will have to file with your State's agency. They can provide you with an application for tax-exempt status (501(c)(3)) which has to be filed with it with the IRS.

Tax Exemption for Nonprofits

Forming a nonprofit corporation with your state does not automatically qualify you for federal tax exemption with the IRS. Tax exempt status can provide complete relief from taxes, reduced rates, or tax on only a portion of items exemption of charitable organizations from property taxes and income taxes, veterans, and certain cross-border or multi-jurisdictional scenarios.

Taxes are special kinds of fees or charges that the government requires people to pay in order to live and work in their state or country. Once you have created your nonprofit by filing the necessary documents with your state, if you want federal tax exemption, you must file a separate application with the IRS. This application is often referred to as the 501(c)(3) application since that is the IRS code section most commonly applicable to nonprofits. In fact, there are more than 20 code sections for nonprofit qualification. Another common one is 501(c)(7), which applies to social and recreational clubs.

Please see below the information required to become a non-profit, and also the "to do list" before you become tax exempt.

The steps vary by state but will generally include the following:

STEP 1.)
Name the corporation, which ensures that your name is unique and permissible. You can do a name search on the website for the **Secretary of State** in your state.

STEP 2.)
Get state tax identification number. You will need to apply for an employer identification number (**EIN**). This is a requirement for all tax-exempt organizations, even if they don't have employees. You can apply online through the IRS website (**IRS.gov**), by phone at 1-800-829-4933, or by mailing in Form SS-4, Application for Employer Identification Number.

STEP 3.)
Prepare and file your **Articles of Incorporation**. The articles of incorporation is the document that creates your corporation. You can also download this form from the secretary of state website. The fee varies from state to state.

STEP 4.)
Appoint one to three directors depending on your needs and state requirements. All corporations must have directors whose responsibility it is to oversee the organization, advise management and make key decisions such as hiring and firing the company's executive officers.

STEP 5.)
Hold a directors' meeting in which you appoint/elect officers and prepare organizing documents and bylaws. Also, start a record book where you keep minutes from this and subsequent meetings.

STEP 6.)
Apply for a **DUNS** number by going to this website: https://fedgov.dnb.com/webform

STEP 7.)
Now you can apply for tax exempt status (501c3) through the IRS in order to receive donations.

**If you plan on receiving less than $10,000 in donations, then the filing fee is $450 **If you plan on receiving more than $10,000 in donations, then the filing fee is $850.

Checklist for New Nonprofit Corporations

Incorporating your nonprofit and obtaining tax-exempt status are just two of many required steps. The following is a list of things to do or consider after starting a new nonprofit corporation.

1. Establish a corporate banking account.
2. Contact the state tax board for information about obtaining a state tax number and see if additional information must be submitted for state tax exemption. Or you can also contact the IRS at https://www.irs.gov/
3. Check with the state Department of Consumer Affairs or Business Licensing to obtain any required business licenses or permits.
4. Contact the state Attorney General's Office to see if registration or reporting is required.
5. Find out about workers' compensation if you will have employees.
6. Protect your trade name. For more information on federal trademark and copyright services as well as fictitious name registration, please go to http://www.uspto.gov/trademarks-getting-started/trademark-basics/trademark-patent-or-copyright.

MISSION STATEMENT

Remember that you will be held to the requirements of your mission statement. Your work ethics and performance will depend on your individual contribution to the organization. If you live up to these mission statement requirements, then you will be a "full" participant in the team. If you do not meet the mission statement requirements, you may be considered a partial participant or non-participant.

You should also have a credible program, service achievements or plans in place that will support your mission.

Whichever business structure that you choose to start, remember that behaving legally represents the first step toward ethical behavior. Ethical behavior reflects proper relationships among people. Certainly, ethical behavior almost always requires obeying legal standards, but that is just the beginning. Ethical behavior involves the broader issues of fairness and morality. **BEST OF LUCK!!!**

REFERENCES:

BANKS, FINANCING, MONEY, YOUTH
In-text: (Banks, Financing, Money, Youth, 2017) Retrieved December 31, 2017 from Canva.com
https://www.canva.com/design/DACrDlE6AP8/F1taWz2-WrLkSi-RAq846g/edit

D&B DUNS Request (n.d.) Retrieved December 31, 2017 from fedgov.dnb.com
https://fedgov.dnb.com/webform/CCRSearch.do?val=1

Employer ID Numbers. (n.d.). Retrieved December 31, 2017, from irs.gov
https://www.irs.gov/businesses/small-businesses-self-employed/employer-id-numbers

Entrepreneur. 2017. In Merriam-Webster.com.
Retrieved December 31, 2017, from https://www.merriam-webster.com/dictionary/entrepreneur

Next Gen Personal Finance: Home. Ngpf.org Retrieved December 28, 2017 from:
https://www.ngpf.org/activities/

Niche. 2014. In Merriam-Webster.com.
Retrieved January 15, 2014, from https://www.merriam-webster.com/dictionary/niche

White, Aspire 2 Acquire, D. (2014). Aspire 2 Acquire Youth Devotional. Raleigh, NC: Aspire 2 Acquire.